The Dismantling of the Chains

Getting Over Depression and Embracing Life

Deepak Singh

ISBN 978-93-5667-719-7
© Deepak Singh 2023

Published in India 2023 by Pencil

A brand of
One Point Six Technologies Pvt. Ltd.
Unit no. 26, Ground Floor, Building A1,
Wadala Truck Terminal Road,
Near Post Office, Antop Hill, Mumbai - 400037
E connect@thepencilapp.com
W www.thepencilapp.com

DISCLAIMER: *The opinions expressed in this book are those of the authors and do not purport to reflect the views of the Publisher.*

Author biography

Hello! Happy to meet you, I'm Deepak Singh. I work as a research analyst and am passionate about writing books and doing research on the planet Earth, space, and the art of living. I most likely have high analytical and critical thinking abilities that enable me to assess data, spot trends, and reach conclusions in my capacity as a research analyst. As part of my job, I might perform primary and secondary research, analyze available data, and provide findings to guide individual, corporate, or organizational decision-making. I adore writing and researching as interests in space and Earth in my free time. You can tell that I have an open mind and am interested in learning about the world around me.

CONTENTS

Introduction

Depression is a crippling mental health illness that affects millions of individuals throughout the world. It can make people feel confined, alone, and hopeless. In "The Dismantling of the Chains: Getting Over Depression and Embracing Life," we strive to share practical solutions and personal tales to assist individuals in overcoming depression and finding hope.

The first chapter begins with an explanation of depression. We define depression, the many types of depression, depression causes, and depression symptoms. We also discuss depression myths and misunderstandings to assist readers in better grasping this difficult condition.

The second chapter digs into the effects of depression. We investigate the impact of depression on mental and physical health, relationships, and work productivity. This chapter emphasizes the significance of tackling depression and the advantages of receiving help.

The third chapter focuses on getting therapy for depression. We talk about when to get help, who to turn to for aid, and what kinds of professional help are available. We also address the stigma of seeking treatment and provide coping skills to assist readers in overcoming this obstacle.

Readers will find solutions for conquering depression in Chapter 4. We investigate lifestyle changes that can promote mental health, cognitive-behavioral therapy, mindfulness-based therapies, and depression drugs. Readers will have a better grasp of the various options available as well as how to select the best plan for their own situation.

Chapter 5 offers the personal accounts of those who have overcome depression. These stories provide insight into the experiences of persons who have overcome depression. Readers will get hope from their experiences and learn how to overcome depression.

The sixth chapter is about finding hope and accepting life. We offer ways for preserving mental health after conquering depression, discovering life's purpose and meaning, and developing resilience to deal with setbacks.

Finally, "The Dismantling of the Chains: Getting Over Depression and Embracing Life" aspires to provide a comprehensive guide for anyone suffering from depression. We provide folks with practical techniques, personal tales, and a message of hope in order to help them overcome depression and live a satisfying and meaningful life.

Chapter 1 Understanding Depression

What exactly is depression?

Depression is a widespread mental health problem affecting millions of people worldwide. It is a mood illness characterized by persistent feelings of melancholy and hopelessness, as well as a loss of interest or pleasure in previously appreciated activities. Depression can be a crippling disorder that impairs a person's capacity to function in everyday life.

A multitude of causes, including biological, genetic, environmental, and psychological factors, might contribute to depression. Depression is frequently caused by a complicated interplay of various causes.

Depression is thought to be induced by a chemical imbalance in the brain, such as serotonin and dopamine. These molecules are in charge of mood regulation, and when they are out of balance, it can contribute to depressive symptoms.

Because of hereditary reasons, certain people may be prone to experiencing depression. Certain genes, according to research, can raise a person's likelihood of developing depression.

Environmental variables such as stress, trauma, and loss can precipitate or exacerbate depression. Poverty, discrimination, and social isolation are among the social and cultural variables that can lead to depression.

Depression can be triggered psychologically by negative thought patterns such as poor self-esteem, pessimism, and feelings of guilt or worthlessness. These cognitive patterns can contribute to a downward spiral of ideas and emotions that perpetuates sadness.

Depression symptoms vary from person to person, but they usually include melancholy, hopelessness, and emptiness, as well as a loss of interest or pleasure in activities. Changes in appetite or sleep patterns, weariness, difficulty concentrating, and feelings of worthlessness or guilt are all possible signs. Suicidal thoughts or behaviors can occur in extreme situations of depression.

Depression treatment usually consists of a combination of medication, counseling, and lifestyle modifications. Antidepressant medication can help to balance the chemicals in the brain that cause depression, whereas therapy can help people identify and change negative thought patterns. Lifestyle improvements such as exercise, healthy food, and social support can also help with depression management.

To summarise, depression is a prevalent mental health illness caused by a range of circumstances. It is a complicated ailment that necessitates a varied treatment strategy. If you or someone you love is suffering from depression, it is critical that you get professional help.

Depression Types

While most people think of depression as a single disorder, there are multiple forms of depression that can affect people in different ways. In this chapter, we will look at the various types of depression, as well as their symptoms, causes, and treatments.

- Major Depressive Disorder (MDD): One of the most frequent types of depression is major depressive disorder (MDD). It is distinguished by a persistent sense of despair, pessimism, and loss of interest in formerly pleasurable activities. People with MDD frequently have problems sleeping, changes in appetite and weight, and difficulty concentrating. They may also experience emotions of worthlessness, guilt, and suicidal ideation. The causes of MDD are unknown, however, it is likely to be a combination of genetic, environmental, and psychological factors. Medication, psychotherapy, and lifestyle changes are frequently used to treat MDD.

- PDD (Persistent Depressive Disorder): Persistent depressive disorder (PDD), also known as dysthymia, is a type of depression that lasts for at least two years. PDD patients have symptoms comparable to MDD patients, but they may be less severe. Individuals with PDD may have low self-esteem, weariness, and difficulties making decisions, in addition to emotions of despair and pessimism. PDD's causes are unknown, however, it is assumed to be caused by a mix of genetic, environmental, and psychological factors. PDD treatment may include psychotherapy, medication, and lifestyle changes.

- SAD (Seasonal Affective Disorder): Seasonal affective disorder (SAD) is a kind of depression associated with seasonal fluctuations. It is particularly common during the autumn and winter seasons when there is less daylight. Low mood, lack of energy, and changes in appetite and sleep patterns are all symptoms of SAD. The specific origins of SAD are unknown, however, it is assumed to be related to abnormalities in the body's circadian rhythm and a lack of sunlight exposure. SAD treatment may include light therapy, medicine, and psychotherapy.

- Depression after childbirth: Postpartum depression (PPD) is a kind of depression that affects women after they have given a child. It is believed that one in every seven women suffers from PPD. Sadness, anxiety, and irritability are some of the symptoms of PPD. Women suffering from PPD may also experience difficulty sleeping, changes in appetite, and difficulties bonding with their newborns. PPD is thought to be caused by hormonal changes, a lack of sleep, and the stress of caring for a newborn. Medication, psychotherapy, and lifestyle changes may be used to treat PPD.

- Bipolar Disorder: Bipolar disorder is a mood condition marked by periods of depression and mania. Individuals experiencing a manic episode may feel elated, have increased energy, and engage in dangerous behavior. During a depressive episode, people have symptoms comparable to those associated with MDD. The causes of bipolar disorder are unknown, however, it is believed to be caused by a combination of genetic, environmental, and psychological factors. Bipolar disorder treatment may include medication, psychotherapy, and lifestyle changes.

In conclusion, Depression is a complex mental health illness that can manifest itself in a variety of ways. Each depression has its own set of symptoms, causes, and remedies. If you or someone you know is experiencing depressive symptoms, it is critical that you seek professional help. Individuals suffering from depression can have healthy and fulfilling lives with the correct therapy and support.

Depression Causes

Depression's origins are complex and multidimensional, and a mix of biological, psychological, and environmental variables are likely to contribute to its development. We will look at some of the most prevalent causes of depression in this chapter.

- Factors of Biology: Several biological elements have been recognized as factors that contribute to depression. One of the most well-known is the dysregulation of neurotransmitters, which are brain chemicals that influence mood. Depression has been linked to a lack of key neurotransmitters, such as serotonin and dopamine. Hormonal imbalances, such as those seen during menopause or thyroid diseases, can also contribute to sadness. Depression development is also influenced by genetic factors. According to research, depression runs in families, and persons who have a family history of the condition are more likely to get it themselves. Some experts believe that some genes may predispose people to depression, while the precise genetic elements involved are not well understood.

- Psychological Aspects: Personality qualities, coping methods, and past experiences are all psychological elements that might contribute to depression. Individuals who have low self-esteem, are highly critical of themselves or have a negative thinking pattern may be predisposed to depression. People who have endured trauma, abuse, or substantial life pressures, such as the death of a loved one, may be predisposed to depression.

- Environmental Aspects: Stressful life experiences, for example, can precipitate the onset of depression. Job loss, divorce, financial issues, or a significant sickness or injury are examples of such situations. Living in a high-stress environment, such as a high-crime neighborhood or a household where there is continual conflict, can also contribute to the development of depression. Substance misuse, especially the use of drugs or alcohol, can aggravate depression.

- Other Medical Issues: Depression can also be a sign of other medical illnesses such as chronic pain, cancer, or multiple sclerosis. These problems can result in physical and emotional stress, which can contribute to depression. Furthermore, certain drugs, such as birth control pills or blood pressure meds, have been associated with depression as a side effect.

To summarise, depression is a complex condition with numerous probable causes. Its development is influenced by biological, psychological, and environmental variables. While we may not be able to totally prevent depression, understanding its causes can assist individuals and healthcare providers in identifying risk factors, implementing preventive measures, and developing successful treatment approaches.

Depression symptoms

A range of factors, including genetics, environmental influences, and personal experiences, might contribute to it. Depression symptoms vary from person to person, and understanding them is essential for recognizing the disease and seeking suitable therapy.

The following are some of the most prevalent depression symptoms:

- Persistent sadness: A persistent feeling of sadness or emptiness that lasts for more than two weeks is one of the defining signs of depression. Feelings of hopelessness, helplessness, and worthlessness may accompany this grief.

- Loss of interest: People suffering from depression frequently lose interest in previously appreciated activities such as hobbies, socializing, and employment. They may also have less sexual urges.

- Weariness: Even after a good night's sleep, depression can cause excessive weariness. This weariness can make getting out of bed in the morning or completing everyday duties difficult.

- Changes in appetite: Depression can cause appetite changes, which can lead to weight gain or reduction. Some depressed people overeat, while others lose their appetite.

- Sleep disorders: Sleep disturbances such as insomnia or hypersomnia (extreme sleepiness) can be caused by depression. People suffering from depression may have difficulties falling or staying asleep, or they may wake up early in the morning and be unable to return to sleep.

- Difficulty concentrating: Depression can impair one's ability to focus, retain information, and make judgments. This can have an influence on employment, school, and other aspects of life.

- Physical symptoms: Physical symptoms of depression include headaches, stomachaches, and back pain. Traditional medical therapies may not be effective in treating these symptoms.

- Irritability: People suffering from depression may be irritable, easily frustrated, and have a low-stress tolerance.

- Suicidal ideation or behavior: Suicidal ideation or behavior can result from depression. If you or someone you know is experiencing these symptoms, it is critical that you seek care right once.

It is crucial to remember that not everyone who suffers from depression may exhibit all of these symptoms. Some people may have only a few symptoms, while others may have numerous. Furthermore, some symptoms may be more severe than others and have a greater influence on daily living.

If you or someone you know is suffering from depressive symptoms, it is critical that you seek help from a mental health expert. Depression is a treatable condition, and with the correct treatment, persons suffering from depression can have happy and rewarding lives.

Depression Myths and Misconceptions

Despite its prevalence, there are numerous myths and misconceptions about depression that might deter people from seeking assistance. In this chapter, we will look at some of the most frequent depression myths and misconceptions.

Myth No. 1: Depression is simply melancholy.

One of the most popular misconceptions regarding depression is that it is merely a state of sadness. While sorrow is a sign of depression, it is not the same as depression itself. Depression is a complex disorder that can cause a variety of symptoms such as feelings of hopelessness, remorse, and worthlessness, changes in eating and sleep patterns, and a loss of interest in formerly enjoyable activities.

Myth 2: Depression indicates weakness.

Another widely held misconception regarding depression is that it is a sign of weakness. This misunderstanding might deter people from getting help and lead to feelings of shame and embarrassment. In actuality, depression is a medical disorder that may affect anyone, no matter how strong or resilient they are.

Myth 3: Depression results from a lack of willpower.

Some people feel that depression is caused by a lack of willpower or an inability to gather oneself. This fallacy is especially dangerous since it can lead to self-blame and intensify feelings of hopelessness and despair. Depression, in actuality, is a complicated disorder with numerous causes, including genetic, environmental, and psychological variables.

Myth 4: Depression exclusively affects adults.

Depression can strike anyone at any age, including children and adolescents. In fact, depression is one of the most common mental health problems among adolescents. However, melancholy in young people is sometimes overlooked or disregarded as normal teenage mood swings. Parents and carers must be aware of the indications of depression in children and seek treatment if they are worried.

Myth 5: The only effective treatment for depression is medication.

While medicine can be an effective depression treatment, it is not the only choice. Other therapies for depression, such as psychotherapy and lifestyle changes, can also be useful. In fact, the most successful way to treat depression is often a combination of medicine and counseling.

Myth 6: Depression is a chronic illness.

While some people suffer from persistent depression, depression is a curable condition for many others. Many people can recover from depression and enjoy full lives with the correct treatment and support.

To summarise, there are numerous myths and misconceptions regarding depression that might keep people from obtaining the care they require. Understanding the true nature of depression and the variety of available treatments can help to lessen the stigma associated with this prevalent mental health disease and ensure that people receive the help they require to recover.

Chapter 2 Depression's Effects

Depression's Impact on mental health

In this chapter, we will look at the effects of depression on mental health and how it can be controlled and treated.

Depression is a complex disorder with numerous manifestations. The most typical symptoms include depression or hopelessness, lack of interest in previously loved activities, changes in eating and sleep patterns, exhaustion, and difficulties concentrating or making decisions. These symptoms might be moderate or severe, and their intensity can change over time.

Depression can have a significant impact on mental health. Depression can cause a wide range of negative emotions, including guilt, shame, and self-blame. They could also experience emotions of worthlessness and low self-esteem. These feelings can be exceedingly difficult to manage, leading to a variety of mental health issues such as anxiety and substance abuse.

Depression can have a substantial influence on physical health in addition to emotional symptoms. People suffering from depression may feel persistent discomfort, headaches, and stomach issues. They may also be more likely to acquire other physical health issues, such as heart disease and diabetes.

One of the most difficult parts of depression is its impact on relationships. People suffering from depression may find it difficult to maintain healthy relationships with friends and family members. They may withdraw from others, leading to feelings of loneliness and social isolation. This can aggravate their symptoms and make recovery more challenging.

Fortunately, there are a variety of depression treatments accessible. Medication and psychotherapy are the most commonly used therapies. Medications can help treat depressive symptoms, while psychotherapy can help people develop coping skills and emotional management strategies. A combination of medication and psychotherapy may be the most effective treatment in some circumstances.

In addition to these treatments, there are a variety of self-care methods that can help with depression management. Exercise, relaxation techniques, and healthy eating habits are examples of such strategies. It is critical to remember that depression is treatable and that treatment is accessible.

Finally, depression can have a considerable impact on mental health, creating a variety of symptoms that can be challenging to manage. However, with the correct treatment and support, depression may be overcome and mental health can be improved. If you or someone you love is suffering from depression, it is critical that you get treatment from a mental health expert.

Depression's Impact on physical health

While many people identify depression with feelings of sadness, hopelessness, and poor mood, the disorder can also cause a variety of physical symptoms that can have an influence on a person's overall health.

Physical symptoms of depression can show in a variety of ways and affect many body systems. Fatigue, changes in appetite or weight, sleep difficulties, and persistent pain are some of the most frequent physical symptoms of depression.

One of the most prevalent physical symptoms of depression is fatigue, which can have a substantial influence on a person's everyday life. Even when they have not engaged in physically demanding tasks, people suffering from depression frequently report feeling weary and lacking in energy. This can make it difficult to concentrate, stay motivated, and complete daily duties.

Changes in appetite or weight are also typical in those suffering from depression. Some people may notice a decrease in hunger and weight loss, while others may notice an increase in appetite and weight gain. These alterations may exacerbate feelings of low self-esteem and negative body image.

Another typical physical symptom of depression is sleep difficulty. Many people suffering from depression have difficulty falling or maintaining asleep, and they may wake up feeling tired or sluggish. This might lead to increased weariness as well as difficulties with focus and motivation.

Another physical symptom related to depression is chronic pain. While the precise association between depression and chronic pain is unknown, it is obvious that the two diseases are linked. People who suffer from depression are more prone to suffer from chronic pain, and the presence of chronic pain can increase depressive symptoms.

Depression can increase the likelihood of having various physical health problems in addition to these physical symptoms. Depression, for example, has been related to an increased risk of cardiovascular disease, diabetes, and other chronic health problems. This is most likely owing to the effect depression can have on lifestyle factors like nutrition, exercise, and smoking.

There are a number of hypotheses as to why depression can have such a negative impact on physical health. One theory is that depression alters the body's stress response system, causing increased inflammation and other changes that might contribute to the development of chronic health problems. Furthermore, depression can impair the immune system, making the body more susceptible to infection and disease.

Overall, it is obvious that sadness can negatively affect physical health. People suffering from depression may experience a variety of physical symptoms, and they may be more likely to acquire other chronic health disorders. As a result, in order to promote general health and well-being, it is critical to address both the mental and physical elements of depression. Therapy, medication, lifestyle modifications, and other interventions focused on enhancing mental and physical health may be used as treatment options.

Depression's Impact on Relationships

Depression can have a negative impact on both the individual suffering from it and their loved ones. In this chapter, we will look at the effects of depression on relationships and how to deal with it.

- The Effects of Depression on Relationships: Depression can have a variety of effects on relationships, depending on the severity of the depression and the quality of the relationship. Here are some examples of how depression can affect relationships:

- Communication Failure: One of the most serious effects of depression on relationships is a breakdown in communication. A depressed individual may feel overwhelmed and unable to speak effectively. They may have difficulty expressing their emotions, opinions, and wants, which can lead to misunderstandings and disputes with their partner.

- Intimacy Loss: Depression can also cause a loss of intimacy in romantic relationships. A person suffering from depression may have poor libido, making physical closeness with their partner difficult. Both spouses may experience feelings of dissatisfaction and disappointment as a result of this.

- Negative Feelings and Thoughts: Negative thoughts and feelings associated with depression include hopelessness, guilt, and anger. These feelings can create a poor atmosphere in a relationship, resulting in increased stress and disagreements between partners.

- Social Exclusion: A depressed individual may become socially isolated and withdraw from their partner and friends. This might result in a lack of support, exacerbating feelings of loneliness and sadness.

- Stress and anxiety levels have risen: Depression can cause increased tension and worry, lowering the quality of the connection. A person suffering from depression may struggle to manage stress and may lash out at their partner, resulting in additional confrontations.

Relationship Depression Management, Managing depression in relationships is difficult, but it is doable. Here are some strategies that may be useful:

- Seek Professional Assistance: Seeking professional counseling is the first step in dealing with depression in relationships. To effectively manage depression, a mental health professional can provide support, counseling, and treatment. They can also provide couples counseling to help with communication and relationship strengthening.

- Communication that is open: Open communication is critical in coping with depression in relationships. Both spouses should make an effort to express themselves honestly and openly. This can help to avoid misunderstandings and confrontations while also promoting a positive environment.

- Self-care is essential: Self-care is essential for dealing with depression in partnerships. Both couples should make an effort to maintain their physical and emotional well-being. This can include regular exercise, a well-balanced diet, and obtaining enough sleep.

- Make a Helping Hands System: Creating a support structure can aid in the management of depression in partnerships. Both partners should make an effort to connect with friends and family members who may offer support and assist with stress management.

- Be understanding and patient: It takes effort and cares to manage depression in relationships. Both spouses should be patient and understanding with one another, and they should avoid assigning blame or passing judgment. This can contribute to the creation of a supportive environment that supports healing and rehabilitation.

In conclusion, Depression can have a substantial impact on relationships, resulting in a breakdown in communication, loss of intimacy, unpleasant thoughts and feelings, social isolation, and increased stress and worry. However, controlling depression in relationships is doable by obtaining professional help, practicing open communication, practicing self-care, developing a support system, and being patient and understanding. Partners can overcome depression and deepen their relationship with effort and dedication.

The Impact of Depression on Productivity and Work

It can have a substantial impact on a person's capacity to function in daily life, including their ability to work productively. In this chapter, we will look at the effects of depression on productivity and work, as well as techniques for dealing with it.

Productivity and Depression

Depression can impair a person's ability to concentrate, focus, and make judgments. It can also cause them to feel tired and unmotivated. All of these elements can have a substantial impact on a person's work productivity. It can also have an impact on their ability to finish duties on time and to a high degree.

Work attendance might also be affected by depression. A person suffering from depression may find it difficult to get out of bed in the morning and go to work. They may also struggle to keep a regular routine or work long hours. All of these variables can contribute to more sick days and lower productivity.

Furthermore, depression might impair a person's capacity to collaborate with others. They may feel lonely or struggle to communicate with their coworkers. It can also have an effect on their capacity to form relationships with coworkers or clients.

Workplace Performance and Depression

Depression can also have an effect on a person's ability to work. A person suffering from depression may struggle to fulfill deadlines, take initiative, or complete work to the best of their abilities. This might result in negative criticism from managers or clients, as well as a drop in job satisfaction.

Depression can also impair creativity and problem-solving ability. A depressed person may struggle to come up with new ideas or answers to difficulties. This can have an impact on their capacity to advance in their careers or take on new challenges.

Workplace Depression Management Techniques

There are numerous techniques for dealing with workplace depression. These are some examples:

- Seek expert treatment: If you are experiencing depression symptoms, it is critical that you seek professional help. A mental health expert can offer you the assistance and resources you require to manage your symptoms.

- Communicate with your employer: It can be beneficial to discuss your situation with your employer. This may allow for adjustments to be made to assist you manage your symptoms at work.

- Take breaks during the day: Taking breaks throughout the day can help you manage your depression symptoms. This can include going for short walks, doing deep breathing exercises, or setting aside time to meditate.

- Set realistic goals: Setting realistic goals for oneself at work might be beneficial. This can assist you in managing your task and avoiding being overwhelmed.

- Create a support network: Creating a support network might help you manage your depression symptoms. Friends, family, and coworkers can all provide support and encouragement.

In conclusion, Depression can have a negative impact on a person's productivity and ability to work. It can impair their ability to concentrate, focus, and make judgments. It can also cause a reduction in creativity and problem-solving ability. There are, however, various ways for managing depression at work, such as getting professional help, communicating with your employer, taking breaks, setting realistic goals, and developing a support network. It is feasible to manage depression while remaining productive at work by applying these tactics.

Chapter 3 Looking for Depression Treatment

Recognizing When to seek help

We all face obstacles or hurdles in our lives that may necessitate the assistance of others. Seeking help, whether for mental distress, physical disease, or a personal crisis, is an important element of preserving our well-being. However, many people are hesitant to seek help because they are afraid, ashamed, or believe they should be able to handle things on their own. This chapter will go over the importance of knowing when to seek help and how to overcome typical hurdles to getting help.

Signs that signal the need for assistance

Recognizing the signals that you require assistance is the first step towards obtaining it. Some of the symptoms that may signal the need for assistance include:

- Feelings of melancholy, hopelessness, or dread that persist

- Sleeping difficulties or changes in appetite

- The use of drugs or alcohol to cope has increased.

- Chronic physical discomfort or sickness

- Relationships with friends or family that are strained

- Difficulties carrying out daily activities or responsibilities

- Suicidal or self-harming thoughts

If you see any of these symptoms, you should seek immediate assistance from a mental health professional or a medical practitioner.

Obstacles to obtaining assistance

Individuals may be discouraged from getting treatment due to a variety of factors, including:

- Stigma: For many people, the stigma associated with mental health and seeking assistance is a substantial barrier. Some people may be embarrassed or humiliated to acknowledge they require assistance.

- Lack of awareness: Many people may not recognise the signals that they require assistance, or they may not know where to turn for aid.

- Financial issues: The expense of mental health treatments or medical treatment can be a substantial obstacle for many people, especially those without insurance.

- Personal beliefs or values: Some people may have personal views or values that discourage them from requesting help from others, believing that they should be able to handle everything on their own.

- Fear of being judged: Rejected, or labeled as "weak" might keep people from getting help when they need it.

Overcoming Obstacles to Seeking Assistance

Overcoming hurdles to getting help necessitates an openness to identifying and addressing them. Some such solutions include:

- Education for oneself: Learning about the benefits of obtaining help and the resources available can make people feel more at ease about seeking help.

- Speaking with others: Talking about one's issues with a trustworthy friend or family member might help lessen stigma and provide emotional support.

- In search of low-cost or free resources: Many towns provide low-cost or free mental health services, and some organizations help people pay for medical treatment.

- Challenging personal ideas: Challenging negative thoughts or attitudes about obtaining help might help people overcome their anxiety or guilt about seeking help.

- Seeking professional help: Individuals enduring emotional anguish, physical illness, or personal difficulties can benefit from professional mental health services.

Finally, knowing when to seek help is an important element of preserving our well-being. Overcoming barriers to obtaining help necessitates a desire to question negative beliefs, educate oneself, and seek help from others. Remember that asking for aid is a sign of strength, not weakness and that there is no shame in requesting help when it is required.

Who can I turn to for help?
Those suffering from depression should seek help from experienced specialists as well as supportive friends and family members. In this chapter, we will look at some of the people and services available to those suffering from depression.

- Mental Health Professionals: Seeking support from a mental health expert, such as a psychologist or psychiatrist, is one of the most effective strategies to deal with depression. These specialists are qualified to identify and treat mental illnesses such as depression. They can provide therapy, medication management, and other forms of treatment to assist people in managing their symptoms and improving their overall mental health.

- Primary Care Physician: For those who are depressed but are hesitant to seek help from a mental health professional, a primary care physician might be a suitable first point of contact. Primary care physicians can offer an initial diagnosis, discuss treatment options, and, if necessary, refer patients to a mental health specialist.

- Support Groups: Joining a support group can be a wonderful method to connect with people who are going through similar depression issues. Individuals in these groups can discuss their experiences, receive emotional support, and learn coping methods in a safe and caring setting.

- Family and Friends: Family and friends can play an important role in assisting someone who is depressed. They can offer emotional support, practical assistance with duties such as cooking and cleaning, and encourage their loved ones to seek professional assistance if necessary.

- Hotlines and Helplines: If you need emergency assistance or are in a crisis, you can call one of several hotlines and helplines. The National Suicide Prevention Lifeline, for example, is a free and confidential program that offers assistance to those in crisis. Other hotlines and helplines may be tailored to certain communities, such as LGBTQ+ people or veterans.

- Online Resources: There are numerous online resources accessible for people suffering from depression. Depression information is available on websites such as the National Institute of Mental Health and the American Psychological Association, including symptoms, treatment choices, and self-care practices. Individuals who are unable to obtain in-person treatment may benefit from online therapy services and mental health apps.

To summarise, there are numerous individuals and services available to those suffering from depression. Individuals must recognize that they do not have to fight depression alone, whether they seek help from a mental health professional, join a support group, or turn to family and friends. Individuals can control their symptoms and improve their overall mental health with the correct help and therapy.

Professional support is available in a variety of formats.

Depression is a widespread mental health problem that affects millions of people throughout the world. Individuals striving to manage and overcome depression can benefit from a range of professional help alternatives. These materials are available in a variety of formats, including treatment, medicine, and self-help resources.

Therapy is a popular professional assistance option for people suffering from depression. Therapists can provide a secure and supportive environment for people to express their thoughts and feelings. Therapists employ a variety of approaches to assist clients in managing their depressive symptoms and developing coping abilities. Individual therapy, group therapy, and online counseling are all options for therapy delivery.

Individual therapy consists of one-on-one sessions with a therapist. Individual therapy allows individuals to work through personal issues while receiving personalized attention and support from their therapist. Group therapy entails a group of people with comparable mental health issues getting together to talk about their experiences and strive toward recovery. Group therapy might help you feel less alone and receive support from others who understand what you're going through.

Another common alternative for people seeking professional help for depression is online counseling. Individuals can interact with licensed therapists using video conferencing or chat platforms when receiving online therapy. This option may be advantageous for those who reside in remote places or who have a demanding schedule that precludes them from attending in-person therapy sessions.

Medication, in addition to counseling, is a professional support option for depression. A healthcare physician can prescribe antidepressant medication to assist manage the symptoms of depression. Medication can be a beneficial tool for those who have severe depressive symptoms that interfere with their daily lives.

Finally, for those seeking professional therapy for depression, there are self-help tools available. Books, websites, and support groups are examples of self-help resources. These resources can provide those with depression information, coping skills, and support from others who have faced similar issues.

To summarise, persons wanting to manage and overcome depression have a variety of professional help alternatives at their disposal. These alternatives include therapy, medicine, and self-help resources, among others. It is critical to locate the appropriate support option for you and to get assistance from a licensed healthcare provider.

Individuals suffering from depression can control their symptoms and enhance their quality of life with the correct expert help.

Managing the stigma of seeking assistance

In this chapter, we'll talk about ways to deal with the stigma of seeking help when you're depressed. To begin, it is critical to understand that seeking help for depression is not a sign of weakness or failure. Depression is a medical disorder that affects people of all ages, genders, and socioeconomic backgrounds. Seeking treatment for depression is analogous to seeking treatment for any other medical problem, such as diabetes or heart disease. It is a proactive move towards better health and well-being.

One of the most difficult aspects of seeking treatment for depression is the worry of being judged or stigmatized by others. Many people assume that seeking help for mental health issues is a show of weakness or should be ashamed of. Individuals suffering from depression may find it difficult to discuss their symptoms or seek therapy as a result of this.

To overcome the stigma of seeking help for depression, it is critical to educate oneself about the problem and the various therapies. When discussing your symptoms with others, this might help you feel more confident and empowered. It can also assist you in understanding that seeking depression treatment is a natural and necessary component of the healing process.

Another method to overcome the stigma of seeking help for depression is to open up about your experiences with others. This can help to remove the stigma attached to mental illness and encourage others to seek help if they are experiencing difficulties. You can also connect with people who are going through similar situations by joining support groups or internet forums.

It is also critical to seek the assistance of a mental health professional who can offer you the support and direction you require to manage your symptoms. Mental health specialists are equipped to assist those suffering from depression and can offer you effective treatments such as counseling and medication.

Finally, keep in mind that recovery from depression is a process. Managing your symptoms and determining the best treatment strategy for you may require some time and effort. However, with the correct support and tools, you can overcome the stigma of getting help during a depressive episode and regain control of your mental health and well-being.

To summarise, seeking help for depression is a courageous and crucial step towards recovery. While mental illness may be stigmatized, it is vital to remember that getting treatment is a natural and necessary part of the rehabilitation process. You may manage the stigma of seeking help during the depression and take control of your mental health and well-being by educating yourself, talking freely about your experiences, seeking help from a mental health professional, and being devoted to your recovery.

Chapter 4 Overcoming Depression Techniques

Changes in lifestyle that can aid

In this chapter, we will look at various lifestyle adjustments that can help with depression management.

- Exercise on a regular basis: Exercise is one of the most effective ways to alleviate depression. Exercise causes the release of endorphins, which are natural feel-good hormones. These endorphins aid in the reduction of stress and anxiety, both of which can lead to depression. Regular exercise also aids in the improvement of sleep, energy levels, and general happiness. Adults should acquire at least 150 minutes of moderate-intensity exercise per week.

- Balanced diet: Eating a healthy, balanced diet can also aid in the management of depression symptoms. Fruits, vegetables, whole grains, lean protein, and healthy fats are all part of a well-balanced diet. Processed foods, sweets, and caffeine should be avoided because they might contribute to mood fluctuations and increase depressive symptoms.

- Adequate sleep: Adequate sleep is critical for controlling depressive symptoms. Sleep deprivation can cause weariness, irritation, and difficulties concentrating, all of which can contribute to depression. Adults should receive 7-9 hours of sleep per night, according to experts.

- Mindfulness and meditation: These practices can also aid in the management of depressive symptoms. These practices aid in the reduction of stress and anxiety, both of which can lead to depression. Mindfulness and meditation can be practiced in a variety of ways, including yoga, deep breathing exercises, and simply sitting quietly for a few minutes each day to focus on your breath.

- Social support: Having a solid support system can also help with depression management. Spending time with friends and family, participating in support groups, and speaking with a therapist can all help to create a sense of community and belonging. Social support can also give you a sense of purpose and help you feel less lonely and isolated.

- Avoiding alcohol and drugs: While alcohol and drugs may provide a short respite from depressive symptoms, they can also increase symptoms and lead to addiction. It is critical to avoid taking these substances as a coping method and, if necessary, to seek professional help.

Finally, implementing lifestyle adjustments can help with depression symptoms. Regular exercise, a balanced diet, proper sleep, mindfulness and meditation, social support, and abstaining from alcohol and drugs are all key lifestyle adjustments that can help to improve overall mood and lessen depression symptoms. However, it is critical to contact a healthcare practitioner to identify the best treatment approach for your specific circumstances.

Cognitive behavioral treatment (CBT)

Cognitive-behavioral therapy (CBT) is a type of psychotherapy that focuses on modifying people's thoughts and behaviors to help them overcome psychological difficulties. It is founded on the premise that our ideas, feelings, and behaviors are all interrelated and that changing one might affect the others.

CBT is a time-limited and structured therapy that normally consists of 12-20 sessions, however, this might vary depending on the individual and the severity of their symptoms. The therapist and client collaborate to establish precise goals and techniques for reaching, them.

CBT begins with identifying the client's negative thoughts or beliefs, which are frequently automatic and unreasonable. These ideas can lead to the emergence and persistence of psychological issues such as anxiety, depression, and phobias. After identifying these thoughts, the therapist works with the client to confront them and replace them with more positive and realistic thoughts.

A person suffering from social anxiety, for example, may have the automatic notion "everyone is looking at me and judging me." The therapist would work with the client to dispute this notion by requesting evidence to support or reject it. The therapist may also teach the client coping tactics like relaxation, exposure therapy, and cognitive restructuring.

CBT focuses on modifying behaviors as well as changing negative beliefs. The therapist collaborates with the client to identify and change maladaptive behaviors that may be contributing to their problems. A person suffering from depression, for example, may shun social situations and activities that they once enjoyed. The therapist would gradually boost the client's activity level and reintroduce enjoyable activities.

CBT has been demonstrated to be useful in the treatment of a variety of psychological conditions, including anxiety disorders, mood disorders, eating disorders, substance misuse, and personality disorders. It has also been demonstrated to be useful in avoiding relapse following treatment.

One of CBT's benefits is its emphasis on the present and future rather than the past. While understanding the causes that contributed to the formation of psychological issues is important, CBT focuses on the present and establishing solutions to overcome current problems.

Another advantage of CBT is that it is evidence-based. CBT has been widely studied and found to be helpful in various trials. Because of this evidence-based approach, CBT is now recommended as a first-line treatment for a wide range of psychological issues.

To summarise, CBT is a time-limited systematic therapy that focuses on modifying negative beliefs and behaviors in order to solve psychological disorders. It has undergone extensive research and has been proven to be useful in the treatment of a wide spectrum of psychiatric issues. Its emphasis on the present and evidence-based approach makes it an appealing treatment option for many people.

Therapies Based on Mindfulness

Mindfulness-based therapies have grown in popularity in recent decades as a means of improving mental health and well-being. These therapies employ strategies that encourage present-moment awareness and acceptance of one's thoughts, emotions, and physiological sensations. They are built on mindfulness concepts, which are the practice of being completely engaged and present in the present moment.

Mindfulness-Based Stress Reduction (MBSR), Mindfulness-Based Cognitive Therapy (MBCT), and Acceptance and Commitment Therapy (ACT) are some of the mindfulness-based therapies that have been established. This chapter will go over various treatments and their uses.

MBSR (Mindfulness-Based Stress Reduction)

Dr. Jon Kabat-Zinn established MBSR at the University of Massachusetts Medical School in the 1970s. It is an eight-week program that teaches mindfulness meditation, body awareness, and yoga as a stress-reduction and overall well-being technique. The program includes weekly two-and-a-half hour sessions as well as a one-day retreat.

Participants in the program learn to be aware of their thoughts, emotions, and bodily sensations without judgment or reactivity. Participants in mindfulness meditation learn to examine their thoughts and emotions as they occur and to let them pass without becoming engrossed in them. This reduces tension and anxiety while also promoting a sense of well-being.

MBSR has been demonstrated in studies to be useful in lowering stress, anxiety, depression, and chronic pain symptoms. It has also been found to increase immunological function and lower the chance of recurrence in people suffering from depression.

MBCT stands for Mindfulness-Based Cognitive Therapy

MBCT was created to help people with depression who have had three or more episodes avoid relapse. It combines cognitive therapy and mindfulness approaches to assist individuals in recognizing and changing problematic thought patterns.

MBCT is an eight-week program that trains participants to recognize and respond to negative thought patterns using mindfulness-based tactics. Participants learn to examine their thoughts and feelings without judgment and to stay present in the moment. They also acquire cognitive skills to aid in the recognition and modification of harmful thought patterns.

MBCT has been demonstrated in studies to be beneficial in lowering symptoms of depression and anxiety, as well as preventing relapse in people suffering from depression.

ACT stands for Acceptance and Commitment Therapy

ACT is a type of therapy that combines mindfulness with cognitive and behavioral tactics. It is predicated on the notion that accepting one's own ideas and emotions is the first step toward creating positive changes.

ACT teaches people to notice their thoughts and emotions without judgment and to embrace them as a normal part of life. It also teaches people how to recognize their values and act on those principles.

ACT has been demonstrated in studies to be useful in the treatment of a variety of mental health disorders, including depression, anxiety, and substance dependence. It has also been demonstrated to increase quality of life and well-being.

In conclusion, Mindfulness-based therapies have grown in popularity in recent years as a means of improving mental health and well-being. These therapies employ strategies that encourage present-moment awareness and acceptance of one's thoughts, emotions, and physiological sensations. They have been demonstrated to be useful in lowering stress, anxiety, depression, and chronic pain symptoms, as well as enhancing immunological function and overall quality of life. If you want to learn more about mindfulness-based therapies, it is best to consult with a mental health expert who can help you choose the best program for your requirements.

Chapter 5 Embracing Life and Finding Hope

How to Find Life's Purpose and Meaning

Finding one's life's purpose and meaning is one of the most fundamental and universal human aspirations. For ages, philosophers, scientists, and thinkers have struggled with this subject. While there is no definite solution to this question, there are numerous approaches and strategies that can assist us in discovering the purpose and meaning of our lives.

- Consider your ideals and convictions: The first step towards discovering your life's purpose and meaning is to examine your values and beliefs. What is essential to you? What causes do you support? What drives you? Take some time to consider and write down the things that are most important to you. This will serve as a beginning point for your search for meaning.

- Investigate your interests and passions: Exploring your passions and interests is another method to discover your life's purpose and meaning. What do you enjoy doing? What activities bring you the most joy? What themes pique your interest?

Pursuing your interests might help you achieve fulfillment and significance in your life.

- Consider your skills and abilities: Consider your assets and talents as another strategy for discovering your life's purpose and meaning. What do you excel at? What do others frequently commend you on? What abilities do you enjoy utilizing? You can choose a career or interest that allows you to fully utilize your skills and talents by focusing on your strengths and talents.

- Volunteering and giving back: Volunteering and giving back to the community can also assist you in discovering your life's purpose and meaning. Helping others can provide a sense of fulfillment and purpose that is difficult to find otherwise. Consider volunteering in your neighborhood or joining a service organization or charity.

- Investigate several employment options: If you are dissatisfied with your current job, it may be time to consider changing careers. Consider your interests and skills, then look for opportunities that correspond with those. You might also seek guidance from a career counselor or mentor on how to choose a career that is relevant to you.

- Reflect on yourself: Finally, practicing self-reflection can be a valuable technique in discovering the purpose and meaning of your life. Every day, set aside time to reflect on your ideas, feelings, and experiences. This can help you become more self-aware and get clarity about your life's mission.

To summarise, discovering one's life's purpose and meaning is a journey that necessitates self-reflection, investigation, and an openness to new experiences. You can find more fulfillment and purpose in your life if you take the time to think on your values, explore your hobbies and interests, consider your abilities and talents, volunteer and give back, explore other career routes, and practice self-reflection.

Developing Resilience and Dealing with Setbacks
Developing resilience is a necessary ability that can assist individuals in navigating life's trials and failures. Resilience is the ability to adapt to stress, hardship, and trauma and recover from adversity. It is a learned skill that may be cultivated with practice and patience rather than intrinsic quality. This chapter will look at ways to build resilience and deal with setbacks.

- Develop a Growth Mindset: Developing a growth mindset is an important step in strengthening resilience. A growth mindset is a concept that your abilities and traits can be improved through hard effort and devotion. This idea can assist you in approaching obstacles with a positive mindset and viewing failures as opportunities to learn and improve. A growth mentality enables you to stay motivated and endure in the face of adversity.

- Create a Support System: Building resilience requires a strong support system. Friends, family, or mentors who can offer emotional support can help you deal with challenging situations. Talking to someone can help you process your feelings and gain perspective on your circumstance. It takes time to build a support system, but it is critical to make an effort to connect with others and form meaningful relationships.

- Self-care is essential: Maintaining resilience requires self-care. Taking care of your physical and mental well-being can aid in stress management and the prevention of burnout. Exercise, a healthy diet, meditation, and engaging in things that bring you joy are all examples of self-care. It is critical to prioritize and practice self-care on a regular basis.

- Setbacks teach us valuable lessons: Setbacks are an unavoidable aspect of life, and they can provide a chance for personal development and learning. When faced with a setback, it is critical to reflect on what occurred and determine what you can learn from the experience. Questioning yourself, "What went wrong?" or "What could I have done differently?" can help you acquire insight into the issue and avoid repeating the same error in the future.

- Concentrate on Solutions: When presented with a problem, it is easy to become engrossed in it and feel overwhelmed. Instead of concentrating on the problem, try to concentrate on finding solutions. Identifying action steps to solve the problem might help you feel more in control and minimize stress.

- Exercise Gratitude: The practice of focusing on the positive parts of life and being grateful for what you have is known as gratitude. Practicing appreciation can assist you in maintaining a happy mindset and developing resilience. Making a habit of jotting down your blessings might help you create a happy mentality and minimise stress.

Finally, cultivating resilience is a talent that can be learned and practiced through time. You may build the resilience you need to navigate life's obstacles with confidence and grace by fostering a growth mindset, creating a support system, practicing self-care, learning from setbacks, focusing on solutions, and practicing thankfulness. Keep in mind that failures are a normal part of life and can provide a chance for growth and learning. You may build the resilience you need to handle any obstacle by being patient and persistent.

Chapter 6 Conclusion

Depression is a difficult mental health issue that affects millions of people worldwide. However, with the correct tactics and assistance, depression may be overcome and optimism restored.

In "The Dismantling of the Chains: Getting Over Depression and Embracing Life" we provide readers with a complete approach to understanding and overcoming depression. We began by defining depression, refuting popular myths and misconceptions, and investigating its causes and symptoms.

We then discussed depression's impact, emphasizing the toll it takes on mental and physical health, relationships, and work productivity. We emphasized the significance of seeking help and provided advice on how to do so.

We offered readers realistic methods for alleviating depression, such as lifestyle modifications, therapy, and medication. We also presented personal tales of those who have struggled with and conquered depression, providing hope and inspiration.

Finally, we concentrated on finding hope and enjoying life. We gave readers tips on how to preserve mental health after conquering depression, how to find purpose and meaning in life, and how to build resilience to deal with disappointments.

Finally, we hope that "The Dismantling of the Chains: Getting Over Depression and Embracing Life" has given readers the tools and support they require to overcome despair and live a satisfying and meaningful life. We want readers to know they are not alone and that there is yet hope for a better future. Remember that with the correct support and tactics, you can break free from the bonds of despair and embrace everything that life has to offer.